Great Artists

Pieter Bruegel

ABDO
Publishing Company

Adam G. Klein

visit us at
www.abdopublishing.com

Published by ABDO Publishing Company, 4940 Viking Drive, Edina, Minnesota 55435.
Copyright © 2007 by Abdo Consulting Group, Inc. International copyrights reserved in all
countries. No part of this book may be reproduced in any form without written permission from
the publisher. The Checkerboard Library™ is a trademark and logo of ABDO Publishing
Company.

Printed in the United States.

Cover Photo: Corbis
Interior Photos: Art Resource pp. 9, 13, 15, 21; Bridgeman Art Library pp. 4, 9, 11; Corbis
    pp. 17, 19, 23, 25, 29; Getty Images pp. 1, 5, 27

Series Coordinator: Megan M. Gunderson
Editors: Rochelle Baltzer, Megan M. Gunderson
Cover Design: Neil Klinepier
Interior Design: Dave Bullen

Library of Congress Cataloging-in-Publication Data

Klein, Adam G., 1976-
  Pieter Bruegel / Adam G. Klein.
    p. cm. -- (Great artists)
  Includes index.
  ISBN-10 1-59679-727-4
  ISBN-13 978-1-59679-727-7
  1. Bruegel, Pieter, ca. 1525-1569--Juvenile literature. 2. Painters--Belgium--Biography--
Juvenile literature. I. Bruegel, Pieter, ca. 1525-1569. II. Title II. Series: Klein, Adam G.,
1976- . Great artists.

  ND673.B73K39 2006
  759.9493--dc22

                                                                          2005017886

Contents

Pieter Bruegel 4

Timeline 6

Fun Facts 7

Mysterious Beginnings 8

Journey to Rome 10

More Adventures 12

Antwerp 14

Painting Peasants 16

Brussels 18

The Months 20

Finding Beauty 22

A New Outlook 24

A Final Request 26

Bruegel's Legacy 28

Glossary 30

Saying It 31

Web Sites 31

Index 32

Pieter Bruegel

Pieter Bruegel was a great artist of the **Low Countries**. He worked during the **Renaissance**. During that time, Michelangelo painted masterpieces, William Shakespeare wrote plays, and Galileo Galilei challenged the world of science. The work of these men and others like them changed the world.

In his artwork, Bruegel presented **allegories**, biblical stories, peasant scenes, and landscapes. Today, Bruegel is known for his meaningful paintings. But in his own time, he was known more for **engravings** that were based on his drawings.

Later in Bruegel's life, King Philip II of Spain took control of the Netherlands.

Very few images of Bruegel exist. This engraving was created after his death.

In a Bruegel painting, the main story is not always the most prominent image. In Landscape with the Fall of Icarus, *the viewer can just spot Icarus's legs in the sea.*

Violence then swept through the area. Bruegel spoke out against Spanish control through his paintings. In good times and bad, Pieter Bruegel reached out to people through his art.

Timeline

1525 ~ Pieter Bruegel was born in Breda, in present-day Netherlands.

1551 ~ Bruegel became a master in Antwerp's painter's guild.

1553 ~ Bruegel painted *Landscape with Christ and the Apostles at the Sea of Tiberias*.

1556 ~ Bruegel created *Big Fish Eat Little Fish*.

1559 ~ Bruegel completed *The Fight Between Carnival and Lent* and *The Netherlands Proverbs*.

1560 ~ Bruegel painted *Children's Games*.

1562 ~ Bruegel completed *The Fall of the Rebel Angels*.

1563 ~ Bruegel created *The Tower of Babel* and *The Flight into Egypt*.

1565 ~ Bruegel created a series of paintings based on the months for Niclaes Jonghelinck.

1567 ~ Bruegel completed *The Massacre of the Innocents*, *Peasant Wedding*, and *The Peasant Dance*.

1568 ~ Bruegel painted *The Parable of the Blind*, *The Misanthrope*, *Peasant and Bird Nester*, and *The Magpie on the Gallows*.

1569 ~ Bruegel died and was buried in Brussels.

- Pieter Bruegel was actually born "Pieter Brueghel." But in 1559, he dropped the "h." His sons decided to keep the "h," so Pieter the Younger and Jan spelled their name "Brueghel."

- Bruegel created three versions of *The Tower of Babel*. The earliest version was painted on ivory. It was part of Giulio Clovio's art collection, but today it is lost. Currently, the two surviving works are held in museums in Austria and the Netherlands.

- *The Way to Calvary* is Bruegel's largest known painting. It is 49 inches (124 cm) tall and 67 inches (170 cm) wide.

- Bruegel's home in Brussels became a museum. However, some people believe the museum planners may have chosen the wrong house!

Mysterious Beginnings

Pieter Bruegel lived during the 1500s. At that time, people did not keep official birth records. So, the exact date of Pieter's birth is unknown. Many people believe he was born around 1525 in Breda, in what is now the Netherlands.

Little is known about Pieter's early life. Some people believe he came from a peasant family. This is because later he became known for his paintings of peasants. But today, most scholars agree that Pieter grew up in a city.

Pieter began his career in Antwerp, in what is now Belgium. There, he became an **apprentice** to painter Pieter Coecke van Aelst. Coecke produced sculptures, stained glass, and **tapestries**. He also worked as an **architect**.

In the early years of his career, Pieter's work looked much different from Coecke's style. But as Coecke's apprentice, Pieter learned about different artistic styles and **techniques**.

Both Coecke and Bruegel painted biblical scenes, but Bruegel usually emphasized the landscape. This can be seen when comparing Bruegel's The Flight into Egypt *(right)* with Coecke's version of the story *(left).*

While Pieter worked for Coecke, he learned about yet another important art form. Coecke's wife, Maria Verhulst Bessemers, was an expert in **watercolor**. Many scholars believe Maria taught Pieter the **technique**.

Journey to Rome

In 1551, Bruegel became a master in Antwerp's painter's **guild**. An artist's work had to be very good to achieve the honor of joining a guild. This promotion meant Bruegel had finished his training. Now, he could set up his own workshop. But Bruegel did not want to open a shop yet.

During the **Renaissance**, painters often traveled to look for inspiration. This way, they also learned from artists in different **cultures**. At that time, Italy was the artistic center of the world. It was a great place for emerging artists to learn more about their crafts. Eager to develop his art, Bruegel decided to go to Italy.

In 1551 or 1552, Bruegel began his journey. During his passage south, Bruegel often stopped to paint and draw. Scholars know that he traveled through France, because he painted a picture of the city of Lyon. For this work, he used **watercolors**.

In Rome, Italy, Bruegel worked with painter Giulio Clovio. A list of Clovio's belongings later showed that he owned several

**Giulio Clovio was known for his miniatures.
Many of these small paintings decorated books.**

works by Bruegel. This included one they had completed
together. Bruegel produced many works in Rome, including
Landscape with Christ and the Apostles at the Sea of Tiberias.
This 1553 work is his earliest signed and dated painting.

More Adventures

Soon, Bruegel felt it was time to go home. On his journey back to Antwerp, he traveled a different path. Again, scholars can follow Bruegel's journey by studying his works. Bruegel made stops in Switzerland. But most important, he passed through the Alps.

In Bruegel's time, there was a demand for artwork of faraway places. Most people could not easily travel, but paintings and drawings allowed them to see other lands. The Alps impressed Bruegel. So, he spent time in Switzerland sketching landscapes.

Bruegel then continued his journey home. But, the scenery in the Alps would inspire him in the future. In fact, many of Bruegel's works featuring this mountain range were completed after he returned from his travels.

Artist's Corner

Today, many of Bruegel's paintings are found in museums. But during his lifetime, they were often owned by individual people. So, not everyone could see his work. In order for his work to be widely distributed, printers made engravings based on his drawings. Because of this, Bruegel first became known for his drawings.

Bruegel's earliest known works are landscapes. The oldest Bruegel drawings that still survive today are of Italy. On his way home from Italy in 1553, Bruegel sketched the Alps in Switzerland *(below)*. Still, Bruegel completed most of his drawings after he returned home from his travels. There, he could combine the various scenes he had witnessed to create the masterpieces that scholars study today.

Antwerp

In 1553, Bruegel returned to Antwerp. Antwerp was a wealthy, successful city. There, Bruegel's career grew. He soon began working for Hieronymus Cock. Cock was an **engraver** who owned a local printing house called At the Four Winds.

Cock enjoyed Bruegel's work, so he **commissioned** drawings. Then, other artists made engravings of Bruegel's designs. Many of the engravings were landscapes based on his sketches of the Alps.

Cock also hired Bruegel to create drawings that included figures. Bruegel completed *Big Fish Eat Little Fish* in 1556. As the name implies, big fish eat smaller fish in this drawing. And, the fishermen eat them all. *Big Fish Eat Little Fish* is an early example of Bruegel's many **allegorical** works. It is also one of Bruegel's most famous images.

Bruegel's work continued to impress people. In 1559, he created two allegorical paintings, *The Fight Between Carnival and*

A proverb teaches a moral lesson. In The Netherlands Proverbs, *Bruegel painted figures acting out individual proverbs.*

Lent and *The Netherlands Proverbs*. *The Netherlands Proverbs* contains examples of more than 100 different peasant proverbs. The painting serves as a visual catalog of proverbs from the area.

Painting Peasants

Painting peasants was one of Bruegel's specialties. It earned him the nickname "Peasant Bruegel." Many of his paintings of peasants were meant to be a social comment on their way of life. The paintings represent entertaining scenes but also try to teach moral lessons. Bruegel studied peasants and their lives to get inspiration for these works.

In 1560, Bruegel painted his next masterpiece. In *Children's Games*, children play in the streets of a village. More than 80 different games have been spotted in the painting. *Children's Games* is just one example of how Bruegel's works capture the lives of many people.

Bruegel studied other topics as well. In 1562, he completed *The Fall of the Rebel Angels*. While it is not a peasant-themed painting, it does focus on morality. This biblical **allegory** shows the fight between good and evil.

There are more than 250 figures visible in **Children's Games.**

In *The Fall of the Rebel Angels*, the people and the creatures are full of movement and energy. Bruegel is known for his fine attention to detail. He is also known for the fantastic creatures he painted. He was influenced by an older artist named Hieronymus Bosch. Bosch also is known for supernatural creations. Artwork in this style sold well at the time.

Brussels

In 1563, Bruegel moved to Brussels, Belgium. There he married Mayken, the daughter of Pieter Coecke van Aelst. They were married at the Church of Notre Dame de la Chapelle.

Moving away from Antwerp affected Bruegel's artwork. Bruegel continued to work for Cock until the end of his life. But while Bruegel was in Brussels, Cock had less influence on his art. Bruegel began to focus less on designs for **engravings** and more on paintings. The move also freed Bruegel to create art in his own style.

Bruegel created several works in 1563, including *The Tower of Babel*. This painting is based on a biblical scene. The tower looks like it was based on **techniques** used in the **architecture** of Bruegel's time.

The same year, Bruegel completed *The Flight into Egypt*. This piece was owned by one of Bruegel's **patrons**, Cardinal Antoine

The Tower of Babel *also looks like it was based on buildings Bruegel would have seen during his visit to Rome years earlier.*

Perrenot de Granvelle. The painting showcases a common theme in Bruegel's work. The landscape appears to be the most important element in the painting, rather than the figures or the story.

The Months

In 1564, Pieter and Mayken's first son was born. They named him Pieter after his father. After this, Bruegel was known as Pieter the Elder. His son was called Pieter the Younger. Pieter the Younger would also become a painter.

The following year, Bruegel completed a series of paintings for Niclaes Jonghelinck. Jonghelinck was a wealthy merchant who became one of Bruegel's most important **patrons**. Eventually, Jonghelinck owned 16 of Bruegel's works.

Jonghelinck **commissioned** a series of paintings based on the months of the year. Bruegel probably made 12 paintings for the series. However, only five of them exist today.

These paintings are similar to the landscapes that Bruegel made after he was in the Alps. They have figures in them, but the people blend in with the land. In fact, they almost become part of the landscape itself.

The Seasons

In each painting in Bruegel's months series, peasants do the work appropriate for that month of the year. *For example,* The Hunters in the Snow (left) *shows people passing the cold month of January by playing on the ice. But, they are also hunting to find food to survive. In the summer months, the peasants bring in the harvest. So,* Haymaking (right) *takes place in July.*

Bruegel worked quickly. He completed the series in just one year! Niclaes Jonghelinck wanted to decorate a room in his Antwerp mansion. So when the paintings were complete, they probably formed a frieze. This decorated horizontal band is sometimes found around the top of a wall or a building.

Finding Beauty

During Bruegel's lifetime, Spain ruled many European countries. These included present-day Belgium and the Netherlands. Spain was trying to enforce a single religion, Catholicism. Bruegel's *The Way to Calvary* speaks out against the Catholic Church. And, it reflects a wish for freedom from Spanish rule.

In 1567, King Philip II sent a new villain into the **Low Countries**. The Duke of Alba and his "Council of Troubles" treated the people there even worse than before. For this reason, the council was nicknamed the "Council of Blood."

That same year, Bruegel painted *The Massacre of the Innocents*, which comments on the mistreatment of people. In the work, Spanish soldiers attack a village. The painting has a biblical theme, but it is set in Bruegel's own time.

Bruegel completed two other paintings in 1567. *Peasant Wedding* and *The Peasant Dance* are more jolly in their subject

With **Peasant Wedding,** *Bruegel shows his concern that people have forgotten they are celebrating a sacred ceremony. Instead, the event has become an excuse to focus on the food and indulgence of a grand party.*

matter. In these paintings, peasants enjoy their celebrations with food and dance. Even though people were suffering, Bruegel still found beauty in the world to paint.

A New Outlook

It looked like happier times were ahead for the popular artist. In 1568, Bruegel's son Jan was born. Jan would also become a well-known painter. That year, Bruegel focused greatly on his work and completed at least five paintings. These included *The Parable of the Blind*, *The Misanthrope*, and *Peasant and Bird Nester*.

The paintings from the end of Bruegel's life show a closer connection to **Renaissance** art. The figures are larger. In the past, Bruegel had painted as if he were observing his subjects from a distance. He still did this in some works, such as the months series. But in others, the landscape became less prominent.

Bruegel continued to make political and moral statements through his work. One of his last paintings was *The Magpie on the Gallows*, from 1568. Some scholars think that the magpie is a symbol to warn others about people that gossip. This was especially important during Bruegel's time, when speaking out against Spain could lead to trouble.

Opposite page: Peasant and Bird Nester

A Final Request

Like his birth, the date of Bruegel's death is not certain. It is believed he died between September 5 and 9, 1569. He was buried at Notre Dame de la Chapelle in Brussels. In his will, he left his wife *The Magpie on the Gallows*.

Some scholars believe one of Bruegel's last requests was that Mayken destroy some of his works. Others say he destroyed some of them himself. It was still a dangerous time in the **Low Countries**. And some of Bruegel's artwork was a challenge to the people in power. Bruegel wanted to protect his family from any danger that his work might bring.

Mayken died in 1578. Jan and Pieter were still young when their parents died. But, they were the beginning of a long history of artists. Painters in the Bruegel family successfully continued the artist's tradition as late as the 1700s.

The Magpie on the Gallows *is about morality. But, Bruegel also focuses the viewer's attention on the landscape. The grand beauty of the landscape contrasts with the small, detailed figures.*

Bruegel's Legacy

Pieter Bruegel stood out from the other painters of his time. The figures in his paintings went against the idealized way that other people painted. Bruegel's figures show a connection between people and nature. These images are meant to entertain and tell stories, as well as teach morals.

Today, nearly 50 of Bruegel's paintings still exist. These few have a great deal of variety to them. They include examples from all of Bruegel's style changes. The surviving works show proverbs, scenery, peasants, and fantasy. Viewers can see both the pain and the happiness that people experienced during Bruegel's time.

Hundreds of years ago, Bruegel's works allowed people to see places they might never visit. Today, people get to make a similar journey. But instead of traveling to a different place, they can travel to a different time.

Opposite page: *Some scholars believe that* **The Storm at Sea** *is one of Bruegel's last works. Others believe it was painted by an artist named Joos de Momper.*

Glossary

allegory - a story or a piece of artwork that teaches a moral lesson using symbolic characters or events.

apprentice - a person who learns a trade or a craft from a skilled worker.

architect - a person who plans and designs buildings. His or her work is called architecture.

commission - a request to complete a work, such as a painting, for a certain person. To be commissioned is to be given such a request.

culture - the customs, arts, and tools of a nation or people at a certain time.

engraving - a print, usually made by cutting designs into wood or metal.

guild - a group of people with common interests, such as painters or merchants, established to help maintain standards of work and protect the interests of its members.

Low Countries - a region in Western Europe that borders the North Sea and includes modern-day Belgium, Luxembourg, and the Netherlands.

patron - one who supports an individual or a cause with money, resources, or influence.

Renaissance - a revival of art and learning that began in Italy during the 1300s, marked by a renewed interest in Greek and Latin literature and art.

tapestry - a heavy woven fabric decorated with detailed designs or pictures.

technique - a method or style in which something is done.

watercolor - a paint made by mixing dye with water.

Saying It

allegory - A-luh-gawr-ee
Antoine Perrenot de Granvelle - ahn-twawn pehr-noh duh grahn-vehl
Giulio Clovio - JOOL-yoh KLAWV-yoh
guild - GIHLD
Hieronymus Bosch - hee-uh-ROH-nee-muhs BAHSH
Lyon - LYAWN

Web Sites

To learn more about Pieter Bruegel, visit ABDO Publishing Company on the World Wide Web at **www.abdopublishing.com**. Web sites about Bruegel are featured on our Book Links page. These links are routinely monitored and updated to provide the most current information available.

Index

A
Alba, Duke of 22
Alps 12, 14, 20
apprenticeship 8, 9
B
Belgium 8, 10, 12, 14,
  18, 22, 26
Bessemers, Maria
  Verhulst 9
Big Fish Eat Little Fish
  14
Bosch, Hieronymus 17
C
Children's Games 16
Clovio, Giulio 10, 11
Cock, Hieronymus 14, 18
Coecke van Aelst, Pieter
  8, 9, 18
commissions 14, 18, 20
F
*Fall of the Rebel Angels,
  The* 16, 17
family 8, 18, 20, 24, 26

*Fight Between Carnival
  and Lent, The* 14
Flight into Egypt, The
  18, 19
France 10
G
Galilei, Galileo 4
Granvelle, Antoine
  Perrenot de 18, 19
I
Italy 10, 11
J
Jonghelinck, Niclaes 20
L
*Landscape with Christ
  and the Apostles at the
  Sea of Tiberias* 11
M
*Magpie on the Gallows,
  The* 24, 26
*Massacre of the
  Innocents, The* 22
Michelangelo 4
Misanthrope, The 24

N
*Netherlands Proverbs,
  The* 15
P
*Parable of the Blind,
  The* 24
Peasant and Bird Nester
  24
Peasant Dance, The 22,
  23
Peasant Wedding 22,
  23
Philip II (king) 4, 22
R
Renaissance 4, 10, 24
S
Shakespeare, William 4
Spain 4, 5, 22, 24
Switzerland 12
T
Tower of Babel, The 18
W
Way to Calvary, The 22